The A   },

the Wonder Pony

Susan C. Perry

METHOW PRESS

Special thanks go to my sister, Linda, for initially giving me the idea to write this book and then painstakingly typing the manuscript, helping with the editing, and collaborating on the illustrations.

1

Young Life

Hi there! My name is Bantry Bay's Erin, but you can call me BB for short. I am a Connemara Pony. Most Connemaras live across the ocean in Ireland, but my parents, Ace and Kerry, lived in the United States. So I was born in Massachusetts, on April 10, 2001.

I have a cute star on my forehead. Some people think that it looks like an upside down map of Texas. What do you think?

Growing up, I spent every day playing in the paddocks at Bantry Bay Farm with my buddies. Paddocks are like little fields with fences around them. When I was three years old, I was trained to wear a saddle and bridle like the grown-up horses wear when being ridden. The next year, when I was four, a nice girl named Paige started to ride me. It sure felt weird when Paige was sitting on my back instead of standing on the ground next to me, brushing my shiny hair.

Paige was a good rider, being very patient with me when I was learning and sometimes confused about what she wanted me to do. But I'm a smart pony, and I quickly learned my lessons: how to walk, trot, or canter when asked to, and how to go in patterns like circles and figures 8s.

2

EVENTING

When I was seven years old, my farm sold me to a teenager named Olivia. I was sad to leave behind my foalhood friends at Bantry Bay Farm when I moved to Hamilton, but Olivia was nice.

Olivia took me to lots of eventing competitions all over New England, and we won lots of pretty ribbons together. Oh, I guess I forgot to tell you what eventing is. This is how it goes.

Most of the ponies who grow up at Bantry Bay Farm compete in a sport called "eventing." It is a sort of like a triathlon. A people triathlon has three different races: swimming, biking, and running. The winner is the person with the fastest total time.

An event competition, a triathlon for horses and ponies, starts with dressage. I think that "dressage" is a French word, which means "training" in English. I have to walk, trot, and canter in a fancy pattern around a ring (like a little arena). I'm supposed to be pretty lively, and also obedient, doing what Olivia asks me to do. Sometimes I don't really want to work that hard and I get lazy, but most of the time I mind my manners and do what I'm

supposed to do. If Olivia asks me to canter next to a certain marker, like the letter "C," I almost always do it right.

After dressage, an event gets more fun, and I get very excited! The second part is called stadium jumping. I get to gallop fast over fancy painted jumps in another ring, without knocking down any of the jump poles. Sometimes I get really excited and buck a little bit, but never enough to make Olivia fall off.

The best part of an event comes last: cross country jumping. It's called that because we get to go out jumping in fields and on trails in the woods. As Olivia steers me into a little pen called the "start box," I am prancing in place with excitement. I can feel my heart pounding inside my chest. The starter man calls out, "5, 4, 3, 2, 1, Have a great ride!" And off we go, blasting out of the start box at a full gallop! Olivia steers me towards the first jump—usually a big log—and

I fly over it. We continue galloping around the 1.5-mile course. We travel up and down lots of hills in open fields and through woodsy trails. We go over about 15 jumps and even go through a small pond of water. It's fun when the water splashes up to my chin.

Every pony gets a score for each of the three sections of the event. The pony with the best total score gets a blue ribbon and a trophy, and lots of carrots. Sometimes that pony is me!

Olivia and I had a lot of fun together. But sadly she kept growing bigger until she was really too big to ride me any more. Off to a new farm.

3

Farm Life

Luckily, I was sold to a really nice lady named Sue. She was older than Paige and Olivia, but not really old. Sue promised me that she would never get so tall that she would outgrow me. I went to live at Sue's farm, Windy Hill, in Upton, still in Massachusetts. It was a really cold day in January when I moved, with huge snowbanks along the driveway and around the barn. The farm really lived up to its name. It sure was windy that day!

Windy Hill is a small farm, compared to where I have lived before. As soon as I got here I fell in love with the stick-your-head-out window at the back of my stall. My new brother is named Cody. He is much taller than me and has huge, strong muscles. He's kind of bossy, often telling me which hay pile to eat from when we are in the pasture. But he's generally a good dude. We became buddies right away.

Cody and I have big stalls with lots of comfy shavings. We spend lots of hours every day out in our 3-acre pasture. Sometimes the grass is really lush, but sometimes it's not. But at least it is something green to eat. I'd always choose grass instead of hay for lunch.

In the winter when there's lots of snow, we have to dig through it to

reach the grass underneath. There isn't much to eat down there, so Sue always puts hay out for us too, on the rubber mats along the fence, so we don't go hungry.

Farm life at Windy Hill is definitely not lonely. There are lots of wild animals that live in the Upton State Forest, right next to our pasture. Smaller animals, like coyotes and foxes, sneak in and out under the fence. Bigger ones, like deer, just jump right over the fence, even though it's really tall, taller than Cody and me! We don't mind sharing our pasture with other animals. There's plenty of space to go around.

There are a lot of birds at Windy Hill too. The outdoor birds, little blue ones, hang out by the bird feeder, where they eat dried meal worms—YUCK—and drink from the shiny birdbath. There are also big black crows and red-tailed hawks that fly by in the sky.

The indoor little birds, gray and brown ones, make nests up near the lights in the barn rafters. They lay eggs in the nests and raise their babies there. The barn birds sure poop a lot! It falls all over the stall walls, and sometimes it even falls on my back. SPLAT!

4

GROOMING

Sue really likes grooming! I do too. Every evening at groom time, she spends a long time working on both Cody and me so we get clean and shiny. Currying comes first. There are lots of different curry tools, some soft and some stiff. I like the stiff one best. Sue scrubs with it in circles all over my body, to loosen up the dirt and dried sweat stuck in my hair. I really love being curried. It feels so good when I'm itchy. When Sue scrubs me by my withers, like your shoulder blades, I stretch my neck way out, turn my head sideways, and twiddle my lips with joy. Ahhhh! Then she uses the soft curry on my face. I love this too!

After currying, when all the dirt is loosened up and I look really messy, Sue uses a brush with stiff bristles to flick off all the gucky dirt. This usually makes the barn floor really messy, as shedded hair and dirt fall off me.

Next comes a soft brush with gentle, flexible bristles. Sue brushes me with the soft brush, in long strokes that go in the direction my hair grows. The soft brush feels nice as it cleans away the last little bits of dirt. It's at this point I begin to shine a little bit. Finally she wipes me all over, nose to tail, with a towel so that I get *really* shiny.

The last step of grooming is combing out my forelock, mane, and tail. I always like my hair to be neatly combed. A messy hairdo is sloppy looking.

I *love* getting treats! Sue puts pieces of carrots or apples in my stall bucket every day, so that I have a treat to eat when I come in from the pasture. Cody gets treats too, of course. After rides we always get a "thank you, good boy" treat like grapes, sugar cubes, peppermints, or a piece of banana. On birthdays and holidays, Sue gives us each a Minty Muffin. Those are our favorites! A Minty Muffin is a soft horse cookie made out of oats and molasses with a peppermint stuck in the middle. YUMMY!

5

OUTINGS

Sue likes to go on "outings" with Cody and me. That means we travel in the trailer to some fun place off the farm to ride outside of the ring. Sue's sister or a friend goes along so there are two horses and two riders. That way we can explore as a foursome. Cody can be kind of lazy sometimes. Even though his legs are a lot longer than mine, he walks pretty slowly. I often have to halt and wait for my big brother to catch up. Sometimes I get a little frustrated that Cody is so slow. I like to go faster.

One of my favorite places to go is a giant field called the Race Course. I think maybe a hundred years ago they might have had horse racing

there, but now it's just wide open hilly fields with lots of cross-country jumps (logs, stone walls, and ditches), like I do in eventing. I may be little, but I am a good athlete, and I can jump pretty high for a pony. I love to gallop all over the Race Course, up and down, and all around. Sue and I go over all the jumps, even the big ones. That's why she calls me the Wonder Pony! My favorite one is the giant pole jump in the corner of the field. We sail over it, both of us smiling wide. Cody doesn't like to jump, so he just watches. I don't know why he doesn't like to jump. He just doesn't.

Sometimes we go to a place called Sandy Neck Beach, on Cape Cod near the ocean. The first time there, I was terrified of the wavy water, and I stayed way up on the top of the beach the whole time. I felt safer away from the scary ocean and closer to the grassy dunes. The second time we went, I was less nervous. Cody was really brave and walked along the edge of the water in the sand. By our third visit to the beach, I followed Cody and got closer to the water. Like I said, I'm a smart pony. I watched Cody and learned that the ocean is not as scary as I first thought.

Every summer, Sue takes Cody and me to her family's farm in Deer Isle, Maine for a two week vacation. It's a *really* long ride in the trailer, almost seven hours, but Cody and I know it's worth it. We have a cute little barn there, with my favorite stick-your-head-out windows.

There's a small grass paddock outside our barn, and it has an apple tree. Our own apple tree! The tree gives us yummy snacks. Because Cody's tall, he can reach up and eat the apples from the branches. I usually eat the ones that have already fallen on the ground. I'm short enough that I can sneak underneath the lower branches and rub my whole body against the tree trunk. That feels so good!

There's a field next to our paddock where Sue and her sister ride us, taking turns on Cody and me. It's nice, but the most fun outing that

Cody and I ever go on is to Acadia National Park, way up north on the coast of Maine. It's a two-hour trailer ride from Deer Isle to Acadia, but it is *so* worth it. Acadia has special trails called "carriage roads." They are really wide and covered with nice crushed gravel. There are no cars, no trucks, and no motorcycles—only bicycles and hikers. Cody and I aren't scared of those. Sue always says how pretty the scenery and views are, but I mostly care about the nice gravel under my hooves—no rocks, no roots, no mud!

The only bad part about the carriage roads in Acadia is that there are actually carriages. Both Cody and I are really scared of the giant horses that pull the big creaky wagons full of people. The horses are OK, but why are they attached to those big noisy things behind them?

6

The Big New Hampshire Event

I said before that I was trained to be an event pony and that I had won lots of ribbons when Olivia rode me. Well, luckily, Sue likes eventing too! It's a lot more interesting and challenging than a plain hunter or dressage show. Sue and I do some of those too, for practice, but the events are so much more fun.

My favorite place to go for an event is the University of New Hampshire. All of the college kids volunteer to help at the event, and the announcer even plays music during stadium jumping! My favorite song is "Wake Me Up Before You Go." It's kind of like my theme song. It helps Sue and me get motivated!

A few years ago, the UNH event was one of our best ever. To be honest, I was kind of lazy in dressage that morning. It was early, and I had not really woken up yet. Sue said that she'd have to carry her whip next time so that I would be more lively. I don't like it when she carries the whip. It stings my side when she flicks me with the whip to get my attention. Because I was lazy in my dressage that day, we didn't get a very good score. We were in 9th place after the dressage section.

Back in my stall, Sue gave me a pep talk. "We can do this, BB," she said. "You're the Wonder Pony! You *love* jumping! You can gallop fast and fly over the jumps in stadium jumping and cross-country." Sue was excited, and I knew she was right. We could gallop fast and fly over the jumps. And we did! We had a clean round in stadium jumping—which means I jumped everything without knocking

anything down, and I went fast. After that we moved up to 4th place.

Then came my favorite: cross-country! There were lots of big jumps and a fun pond with splashy water. I galloped really fast and flew high over every jump. Another clean round! And guess what! That moved us up to first place!

Back at the barn Sue hugged me and cried tears of joy. "We did it, BB! We did it!" We won a big shiny blue ribbon and a special blanket for me with fancy embroidered letters and tiny horse pictures on it. I was so proud of winning that event!

Sue and I have been a pair for a long time now, and we've won several national level awards in eventing. Those are really big. We have lots and lots of other ribbons too. Sue hangs most of our ribbons in the house, but she puts up a few in the barn too. I like to look at then while I'm munching my hay, and remember the fun events.

7

CONNEMARA BREED SHOW

Both Sue and I really like to do a variety of different things. We don't like to do the same thing day after day. That would be boring. We ride in the ring, go on outings to big fields, do trail rides, and do different kinds of competitions. Every July we go to South Woodstock, Vermont for the Connemara Breed Show. Remember, I'm a Connemara pony. Anyway, the show is full of a hundred ponies that are all Connemaras like me. I'm brown, but lots of them are gray or buckskin colored. We're all very smart ponies. Connemaras can learn how to do almost anything!

Our favorite stall in Vermont is number D-18, on the side of D barn where there is a brook. Stall D-18 has warm sun in the morning, cool shade in the afternoon, nice air flowing above the walls, and of course a stick-your-head-out window, which I love. Several bubbling brooks run through the grounds. At the end of every show day, I get to go wading in the brook. Sue wears her tall rubber boots and brings a big sponge so she can give me a wash down with the cold brook water. It feels really refreshing after a long hot day.

At this show, we always compete in a little bit of everything over the two days we are there. There are lots of different fun classes, like in-hand, equitation, pleasure, hunters, jumpers, and dressage. My favorite Saturday class is called "Fitting and Showmanship." It's an in-hand class, which means Sue doesn't ride me but instead leads me around the ring with just my bridle and no saddle. Before this class, Sue gives me an extra special grooming, trims all the scraggly hairs on my legs, and gives my hooves a special oil polish. I look wonderful!

I try my best to mind my manners in the show ring while the judge is watching, by walking or trotting willingly next to Sue while she loosely holds the reins of my bridle. I am supposed to match her pace exactly. When Sue stops, I halt right away and stand with my feet lined up like four corners of a rectangle. I know that I must stand perfectly still while the judge walks around me and looks at me and inspects me to see how clean and tidy and well-mannered I am. Sue and I are really good at this, and we win lots of blue ribbons in Fitting and Showmanship.

My favorite Sunday class at the Connemara show is called Dressage Trail. It is really fun but kind of hard too. We train a lot for it at home at Windy Hill before the show. In Dressage Trail, I walk and trot and do fancy patterns, and along the way there are obstacles to navigate, like poles to go through and things to pick up and put down. My favorite obstacle is the "Jolly Ball Carry." It goes like this:

- From a walk, we halt at a big blue barrel.

- Sue leans over the top of the barrel and picks up the rubber Jolly Ball (a big purple ball like a basketball, but with a handle).

- Carrying it by the handle using one hand, she puts both reins in her other hand and asks me to trot. I do, because I'm a good pony.

- We trot a big circle going left, and Sue steers me with just one hand. I try hard to follow her direction and make the circle round.

- We halt at the end of the ring, at the letter "C" on the fence, and Sue drops the ball into a tub on the ground. I stand still when she does that, even when the ball bounces a little.

- Then Sue holds the reins back in both hands and we trot on.

Sue and I really ace Dressage Trail every year at the show because we practice a *lot!* And usually we win the blue ribbon in this class too. It's almost as fun as eventing, but not quite.

8

Still Happy Together

Time goes by for all of us. I'm getting older now, and so are Cody and Sue. Old age makes me kind of stiff in my joints. When I go out for a ride, it takes my legs a while to loosen up when I start trotting. We may be a little sore in our bodies, but being old also makes us wise in our brains.

I still spend hours every day looking through my big beautiful stick-your-head-out stall window, watching the birds and other animals outside. Sue always remembers to give me a Minty Muffin treat on my birthday (on April 10th, remember!). And while we can't do all the big jumps and events that we used to do, Sue and I still have a lot of fun together every day. There's always a good grooming for me every evening after I have rolled in the pasture. Sue doesn't care how dirty I get; she curries and brushes me until I shine. And puts pieces of carrots and apples in my bucket every night, and whispers, "I love you, Wonder Pony."

Acknowledgements

Many thanks are due to all who helped me with this project. My sister, Linda Kimbrell, suggested that I write BB's story as a fun way to occupy myself during recovery from an injury, and introduced me to Thea Han, who did all of the beautiful illustrations. My test readers gave valuable input: young Elsa Fudeman and her mother Sarah Summers, the director of the Dana Hall School Riding Center; tutor and teacher Laurie Ulmer; international event rider and author Will Faudree; Olympic event rider and coach Bobby Costello.

Thank you to all the instructors and students at the Dana Hall School Riding Center in the 1970s, who taught me the horsemanship skills that I still use every day. And most of all, thanks to those who coached BB and me to all of our competitive wins over the past dozen years: Cookie DeSimone, Sarah Summers, and Bobby Costello.

About the Author

Sue Perry is a Certified Veterinary Technician and equine massage therapist. She lives in Upton, MA with three equines and two house cats. With her Connemara pony Bantry Bay's Erin (BB), Sue has travelled all over New England for cross-country rides and countless successful competitions in a variety of disciplines. Formerly, she was a contributing writer for an equine journal. This is Sue's first children's book.

About the Illustrator

Thea Han is a 12-year-old artist who lives in Halifax, Nova Scotia. In addition to school, she spends her time sailing, skiing, and creating art. Over the past four years, Thea has been honing her art skills in a variety of media, including watercolor, colored pencil, painting, sketching, charcoal, digital, inking, pastel, and more. She has two brothers who don't enjoy drawing but are always impressed by her work. This is Thea's first published work.

CPSIA information can be obtained
at www.ICGtesting.com
Printed in the USA
BVHW012325090223
658229BV00014B/194

9 781736 653746